PRAISE FOR TENIQUA BROUGHTON

"Without a doubt, Teniqua is a visionary leader who leaves an indelible mark wherever she goes. Her ability to navigate complex systems and translate ambitious ideas into impactful results is truly unmatched. Through her work as a non-profit executive, board leader, and social innovator, she's honed a unique leadership style that cultivates diverse, collaborative teams where every voice is heard and valued. But what sets her apart is her genuine empathy and authenticity. She has a remarkable ability to connect with people on a deeper level, building trust and inspiring collective action. In a world desperate for authentic and results-driven leaders, Teniqua stands out as a beacon of hope, an architect of positive transformation."

– Will James, Board Chair,
The State of Black Arizona

"I first met Teniqua when she gave a presentation about the nonprofit she was directing, called **Act One**. I was so impressed with her dynamism and vision, that was also grounded in the real world. I approached her, and for the next ten years we have regularly talked about her endeavors and life. In those ten years, I have watched Teniqua develop the State of Black Arizona and her own consulting business, Verve Simone, and witnessed the unique elements she brings. She has an innate ability to get people talking and addressing touchy topics of diversity and leadership that are real and intimate versus safe, typical conversations–which then brings about impactful change. And at the same time, she brings her passion for the arts and how it is woven into the fabric of all things. She also knows how to build and develop organizations that are grounded in what they do best and how they can do better. She is a mover and shaker and it has been a great privilege to know her."

– Gail Watchel,
Nonprofit Leadership Advocate

"Through her leadership role as chair of the WESTAF board of trustees, Teniqua Broughton has fostered and advanced an extraordinary sense of community and belonging throughout the organization. She has a special way of inviting everyone into the conversation, one that is always infused with patience, honesty and tenderness. Teniqua is as committed to guiding each individual, as she is skilled in leading the whole group. Her inclusive approach generates a sense of trust, belonging and collaboration, creating an environment where everyone feels valued and empowered to show up, check-in, and contribute their best. Her skilled facilitation style, often bolstered with thoughtful visualizations, enables groups to navigate through complex topics like equity, identity, and social justice with enduring grace and building confidence, towards a place of deep meaning and shared understanding."

— Christian Gaines,
Executive Director, WESTAF

"I've had the privilege of knowing Teniqua Broughton for over 15 years, during which time I've not only been a consultant alongside her but, more significantly, a witness to the remarkable leader, poised innovator, and powerful change agent she embodies. Teniqua's dynamic approach to leadership is characterized by her unwavering poise, innovative spirit, and the transformative impact she has on those around her. Beyond professional collaborations, Teniqua is a cherished friend, and it's a joy to contribute to her book, celebrating the inspiring journey of a true leader and trailblazer."

– *Tiffani Davis,*
Education Consultant

"As the little sister, I have known Teniqua Broughton all my life. Since I was born, my sister has gone off to college. Then I got to know my sister a little more when I came to Arizona. I witnessed her growth, her strength, her leadership, and so on. I always admire her leadership in the community. She puts her heart and soul into everything she does. She handles things with grace and kindness. I am so proud to be her sister. She taught me so much. She broadened my horizons and taught me to be open-minded. One thing I will say about Teniqua is that if you look up the word leadership, it will describe her. What you see is what you will get. Teniqua, I am so proud of you, and I love you, sis."

– *Deja Broughton,*
sister to Teniqua

MY LEADER, MY SELF

Self-Aware Leadership for Harnessing Super
Powers in Yourself and Others

By

Teniqua Broughton,

Speaker, Nonprofit Executive and Leader

My Leader, My Self

Self-Aware Leadership for Harnessing Super Powers in Yourself and Others

Copyright ©2024 Verve Simone, LLC.

https://www.vervesimone.com/

All rights reserved. No part of this publication may be reproduced, stored in a retrieval system, or transmitted by any means: electronic, mechanical, photocopying, recording, or otherwise without the author's prior permission except as provided by USA copyright law. To do so is a direct infringement on the author's copyright and intellectual property.

Published in the United States of America by Rich Pageant Media, LLC. (first edition).

Writing Assistance: Anne McAuley Lopez, Agency Content Writer, LLC.

Editing and Preparing for Publication: Christine Leninger, Rich Pageant Media, LLC.

ISBN: 9798326293398 *(Paperback)*

ISBN: 9798326293398 *(Ebook)*

ACKNOWLEDGEMENTS

I wish to acknowledge the remarkable individuals who have not only breathed life into my own but have also generously shared their light, inspiration, along the way.

I extend my deepest gratitude to my mom, Rose Broughton and the incredible women who have served as second mothers, inspiring mothers, and pillars of motherly support throughout my life. Their unwavering guidance, love, and nurturing have shaped the person I am today. These remarkable individuals exemplify the immeasurable value of maternal figures, whose influence extends far beyond biological ties, nurturing not only individuals but entire communities with their wisdom and compassion.

To Gail Koshland and the countless women and men who have stood as advocates and supporters of my leadership journey, I express my heartfelt appreciation. Their belief in my abilities, their encouragement, and their willingness to champion my cause have been instrumental in propelling me forward, fostering growth, and amplifying my impact. Their advocacy underscores the profound significance of having allies who uplift and empower us to reach our fullest potential.

I am forever indebted to Colleen Jennings-Roggensack and the extraordinary women and men who have served as career warriors, recognizing and nurturing my talents even in moments of self-doubt. Their discerning eyes and unwavering support have been a guiding light, illuminating paths I may not have otherwise ventured upon. Their ability to see potential where I may have overlooked it highlights the transformative power of mentorship and guidance in unlocking our true capabilities.

My heartfelt thanks extend to Tiffani Davis and the remarkable women who have cherished authentic friendships, standing by me through thick and thin. Their unwavering support, camaraderie, and shared experiences have provided solace, strength, and laughter during life's trials and triumphs. These cherished bonds underscore the profound value of genuine friendship, offering sanctuary for growth, reflection, and transformation.

Finally, I reflect on the invaluable lessons and learning gained from leading the State of Black Arizona's African American Leadership Institute (AALI), where the journey of leadership intertwines with self-awareness. Through this experience, I have come to understand the transformative power of servant leadership, the importance of fostering a culture of inclusion and collaboration, and the profound impact of leading with authenticity and empathy. These values underscore the essence of effective leadership, where growth, resilience, and collective progress flourish in an environment of mutual respect and shared purpose.

In gratitude and reflection,

Teniqua

DEDICATION

"Be bold. Envision yourself living a life that you love."

– **Suzan-Lori Parks**

This book is dedicated to my mom and dad, Rose and Joseph Broughton. Your unwavering support, guidance, and love have been the cornerstone of my journey towards resilience. Through your nurturing presence and steadfast encouragement, you've instilled in me the strength to navigate life's challenges with determination and grace. This dedication is a testament to the profound impact you've had on shaping my resilience and shaping me into the person I am today. Thank you both.

Contents

PRAISE FOR TENIQUA BROUGHTON i

ACKNOWLEDGEMENTS vii

DEDICATION ix

PREFACE - MY VOICE IS MY SUPERPOWER xiii

CHAPTER 1 - NAVIGATING YOUR LEADERSHIP JOURNEY 1
   How People See You 3
   Vs, Cs, and Gs 4
      What makes a leader? 5
      Becoming Unstoppable 6

CHAPTER 2 - UNVEILING YOUR EXPERTISE 9
   What qualifies me? 10
   Leadership with Impact 12
      Questions for Reflection 13

CHAPTER 3 - DEFINING YOUR APPROACH WITH PRECISION 15
   Three Dimensions of My Approach 17
   Self-Reflection 18
   Self-Awareness 18
   Self-Evaluation 19
      My Self Evaluation Checklist 19
      Questions for Reflection 20

CHAPTER 4 - IDENTIFYING AND LEVERAGING YOUR ZONE OF GENIUS 23
   Discovering Your Zone of Genius 24
   Embracing Your Zone of Genius 26

    Four Strategies to Secure Your Spot in the Room 26

        Questions for Reflection 27

CHAPTER 5 - LEVERAGING YOUR CONNECTIONS 29

    The Relationship Couch 31

    How does your network work for you? 32

        Questions for Reflection 35

CHAPTER 6 - GUIDING PEOPLE AND TEAMS 37

    One-to-One or None 37

    Next is Coaching 39

    Leading Volunteers 40

    Leading a National Team 41

        Questions for Reflection 44

CHAPTER 7 - HANDLING CHALLENGES WITH GRACE 45

    The 24-Hour Rule 48

    The Diamond Leader 50

        Questions for Reflection 51

CONCLUSION - MY LEADER, MY SELF 53

ABOUT THE AUTHOR 55

PREFACE

MY VOICE IS MY SUPERPOWER

> "I come in peace, but I mean business."
>
> – Janelle Monae

As I embarked on the journey of authoring this book, a profound realization dawned on me — each of us possesses a unique voice, making us leaders in our own right because we each come from different places and spaces. At any juncture in our professional journey, we must pause, reflect on our current standing, trace our path, and envision our future. This book is a collection of my reflections, encapsulating the best practices I've gleaned for harnessing the potency of your voice as your superpower, fostering your growth as a leader.

It wasn't always evident that my words carried influence — the way, when, and if I chose to articulate them held power. My voice emerged as my superpower.

And so is yours.

As a small business owner and nonprofit leader, I've encountered many individuals who were hesitant to wield the strength of their voices. There's potency in choosing silence selectively; it can magnify your impact when you decide to speak. Even in my quiet moments, I refuse complicity. I reserve my voice for when it matters most, when there's an audience ready to absorb my message.

Using your voice means acknowledging your capability to impact people, situations, and crucial moments. It involves wielding your voice to convey messages on challenging subjects or during stressful junctures. The difficulty of being heard should not deter you from speaking up.

There are instances where silence can detrimentally affect the community. Advocate for the underrepresented, overrepresented, and those unaware of what they don't know. Speak for those who lack a voice. This is indispensable in narrating your story with conviction. Your voice is, without a doubt, your superpower; employ it judiciously.

Raise your voice when a community is being excluded, intentionally or unintentionally. Shed light on the unmet needs or overlooked opportunities.

Finding solace in my voice as a superpower has been transformative, especially when fortified by facts and lived experiences. The impact is palpable whether I express my truth at a public event or wait for a more opportune moment. Sometimes, a smaller setting proves more receptive to a particular message — as it has been said, honey often attracts more bees than vinegar.

Your voice carries weight.

Let your words mirror the necessary actions to propel a community or situation forward. Occasionally, the outcomes of speaking up may surpass your expectations, yielding different, even superior, results. Recognizing the need and ensuring it is addressed, even if the resolution differs from your approach, is a testament to your influence.

Equally significant is the ability to listen, a superpower in itself. Silence does not denote apathy; it signifies discernment, an understanding that now is not the time to speak. Consider the setting — a smaller group or a one-to-one meeting might be more conducive to effective communication. Reading the room and strategically balancing speaking and listening enhance the impact of your voice.

Acknowledge that you might not always be the most suitable messenger. Sometimes, letting someone with a more influential voice convey the message aligns better with your brand and mission. This isn't relinquishing power; it's strategic messaging.

Networking and connections play a pivotal role. I assume varied roles in different contexts — a nonprofit leader, an arts and culture professional, or a business owner. Tailoring my communication based on the audience, timing, and content is strategic, and you can employ a similar approach to maximize your superpower.

Using your voice is not confined to isolated moments; it's about building bridges, fostering communities, and forging connections. It entails reconstructing fractured relationships or partnerships for the greater good. It requires astuteness in knowing when to yield and when to speak up, understanding that a smaller meeting may be the wisest choice.

Your voice is undeniably your superpower. Use it wisely.

CHAPTER 1

NAVIGATING YOUR LEADERSHIP JOURNEY

> "Great people do things before they are ready. They do things before they know they can do it. Doing what you're afraid of, getting out of your comfort zone, taking risks – that's what life is."
>
> – **Amy Poehler**

Regardless of your chosen path, there is inherent power in steering your narrative. I've faced challenges at various junctures in my professional life, and through learning and self-reflection, I've realized that life is a canvas shaped by my actions. This is my journey, and yours is uniquely yours.

We each come from diverse backgrounds, cultures, and neighborhoods, which means our experiences differ significantly. It's important to acknowledge and respect each other's positionality, while understanding and embracing the unique differences and similarities among us. We all have our families, traditions, education, and life experiences, and as leaders, these aspects greatly influence how we serve others.

Being aware of our own backgrounds and recognizing the diversity in culture and upbringing goes a long way in how we present ourselves and communicate with others. As leaders, our effectiveness in different communities depends on understanding the specific needs and preferences of those we serve. It takes understanding to fit in and make progress with your community. What might work well in one city might not resonate with another, and adapting our approach accordingly is essential for making progress.

Listening attentively and being mindful of how we interact with others can significantly impact how we are perceived as leaders and how we perceive those around us. Taking the time to get to know the people in our community and workspace is important, as they can teach us valuable insights while we share our own experiences with them. By fostering mutual understanding, we can collaborate in ways we might never have imagined possible.

Consider this: How does your background influence how you see others? How do others see you? How do you want your voice to influence others? What message do you convey when utilizing your voice as a superpower? How do you envision your presence in your own life? What defines your professional brand? How do you aim to evoke emotions through your work? Furthermore, how do you perceive yourself and your contributions? By delving into these questions, we embark on navigating our leadership path.

How People See You

Throughout my journey, I've recognized that people, often driven by habit, perceive me through a particular lens. Whether good or bad or somewhere in between, knowing how people see you is good. Maybe we make changes to how we're working. Maybe we appreciate the praise. Maybe we change how we see ourselves.

When I was on the Board of the thriving large nonprofit in Phoenix, a colleague was attending an event that the CEO was also attending. Later, that colleague who had overheard the CEO's conversation praising my work with someone else shared what they had heard. I was surprised that my name was brought up and that the CEO was so impressed by my work. I hadn't realized I had made an impression on leadership! Most of the time, it feels like we are only praised when we are in the room, so it was a good realization that I was appreciated even when I wasn't standing nearby.

The CEO didn't need to say anything about me, but he did. He saw me in a light I hadn't seen myself in. My colleague didn't need to tell me what they heard, but they did. How we see ourselves is often different than how others see us. Listening to the positive things said about me helped me claim the space I didn't know was mine to take, which felt good. It made me feel like my work matters, and my accomplishments are noticed.

We commonly initiate our journey in spaces where we excel or where our parents or teachers believe we excel. However, the trajectory of finding our way encompasses more than mere proficiency. Over time, I have transitioned to a space where my skills, experiences, and education converge, creating a brand authentically representing ME.

Creating a brand that is uniquely YOU is not only possible but essential.

Vs, Cs, and Gs

Whether your aspirations are personal or professional, contemplate what you desire, why, and the sustainability of that aspiration. Here's where I introduce the three Vs:

- **Vision:** Define your future specifically. Where do you see yourself?
- **Variety:** Break out of your comfort zone. Achieve your goals by embracing diverse jobs, volunteer opportunities, and experiences.
- **Vitality:** Identify the driving force for change within yourself or your work. If the changes align with your vision, they are vital for your leadership growth.

It's essential to recognize that not everyone shares the same vision as you, and others may perceive you differently than you perceive yourself at any given time.

Early in my career, I worked in a specific industry and role. Mine was a public-facing role in arts education in schools. People knew my arts integration work was a passion and visible, and needed at the time. Understanding the role arts played in schools was a national concern. We were asking how to integrate it into education. We knew English teachers were using the arts but wanted to know if and how a Math teacher could do that. I was, and still am, passionate about integrating arts and education.

After a while in this position, my peers asked me to participate in arts-related events. They didn't realize that my passions included other areas as well, I craved variety. In my journey, there was a tendency to pigeonhole me as the "arts education lady," even now, 15 years later, I aspired to be more—a leader in finance, for instance. Others might not see you in roles you envision for yourself, and that's a challenge I've grappled with, but stepping out and putting yourself in those roles or opportunities where you can explore is where you (and others) can expand their vision.

After the education job, I took a position at a nonprofit organization, working with kids using art therapy as the medium. In this position, I was leading a team. This gave a better view to my leadership and management style beyond the arts. I began seeing myself as a leader and moved on to positions where I am a leader outside the arts sector, leading me to consulting and working with nonprofit organizations.

What makes a leader?

In my work within nonprofit organizations, I prioritize the three Cs: culture, change management, and co-creation. Understanding the organization's culture is essential for managing changes and fostering sustainability. If any of these components falters, addressing it becomes a priority.

The same principles apply to nonprofit equity, where I develop strategies for reaching specific audiences. We must comprehend the organization's culture before initiating any action. Understanding change management is crucial for addressing challenges, and co-creation becomes paramount when faced with a cultural shift.

If your organization has not included a particular group in its culture, you can only effect change for individuals who are not part of the dialogue. Inviting them to the table for co-creation is imperative to implement meaningful and inclusive strategies with your team.

Becoming Unstoppable

Lastly, the secret to becoming an unstoppable force as a leader is the three Gs: grit, guts, and grace.

When it comes to having grit, it is your never-give-up attitude. You're staying strong and determined, even when things get tough. Leaders with grit don't let obstacles knock them down. Instead, they roll up their sleeves and keep pushing forward, inspiring others with perseverance.

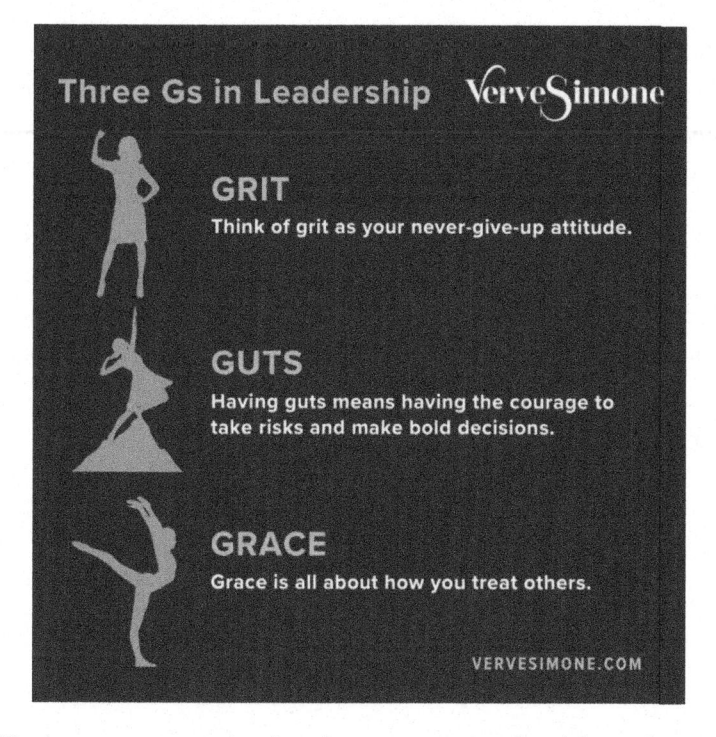

Three Gs in Leadership — VerveSimone

GRIT
Think of grit as your never-give-up attitude.

GUTS
Having guts means having the courage to take risks and make bold decisions.

GRACE
Grace is all about how you treat others.

VERVESIMONE.COM

Having guts means having the courage to take risks and make bold decisions. As a leader, you're stepping out of your comfort zone and facing challenges head-on. You aren't afraid to speak up, make tough calls, or challenge the status quo. You lead confidently, even when the path ahead is uncertain.

And finally, you have grace. You treat others with empathy in a humble and emotionally intelligent way. Graceful leaders build strong relationships, listen to others, and create a supportive environment where everyone feels valued. They lead with kindness and respect, inspiring loyalty and trust among their team.

When combined, grit, guts, and grace make you a strong, unstoppable leader. You inspire others, overcome obstacles, and create a positive impact while staying true to yourself and your values.

As leaders, we must take our own experiences as well as those of others into consideration because those are part of what defines us as humans and as leaders. We can also combine what the 3Vs and 3Cs mean for your organization so that leaders and team members are focused and ready to build a successful, mission-driven organization.

CHAPTER 2

UNVEILING YOUR EXPERTISE

> "Whoever you look up to, or put on a pedestal, know that they have fears, too. They just learned how to push past it."
>
> – Leila Ali

Individuals frequently inquire whether I can guide them in navigating their leadership journey. They desire to emulate certain admirable aspects; having witnessed me speak at an event or facilitate a meeting or workshop, emulation is commendable. We must acknowledge that each of us treads a distinct path.

As I sit here, I ponder what qualifies me for my role. What credentials make me apt to lead teams and workshops? What attributes define me as a speaker and nonprofit leader? Chances are, you've grappled with similar inquiries. The key lies in cultivating self-awareness.

Looking back on my leadership journey, I discovered I had clear goals at nearly every juncture. What about your personal and professional development plans? What validates your competence in your current pursuits? Take action by journaling about your journey thus far.

When I recounted my career, I realized where I had evolved, learned, and now share my experiences. Retrospection is an ongoing process that allows us to gauge our present standing against where we were a month, six months, a year, or even many years ago.

Throughout my career, mentors and role models have played pivotal roles in shaping my identity. Experiences and conversations have sprouted personal and professional growth within me. I often find it challenging when younger and less experienced individuals label themselves consultants. It's hard for me to fathom how they possess the life experience needed to foster career growth for those more seasoned in the workforce. Becoming a consultant is a title earned through a wealth of experiences with diverse people in various settings.

What qualifies me?

I am qualified as a speaker, workshop facilitator, leader, and more because I have been unwaveringly committed to personal and professional growth over the last two decades. During this period, I've undergone significant self-development and substantially impacted communities in Arizona and across the country. My qualification stems from embracing the responsibility of delivering value, whether stepping in as an employee, board member, or volunteer.

The Monarch Council at the Desert Botanical Garden in Phoenix, was an initiative focused on an age diversification strategy I founded when I was on the board. This strategy focuses on engaging people 40 years of age and younger, a population desired by the garden listed on their master plan but needed to be led by the individuals in that age group. This strategy is still sustained, and I am proud of that.

A current program is the State of Black Arizona's African American Leadership Institute, which was acquired from another nonprofit in 2017, in which I have been involved with since 2015. This is an important institute in Arizona because it is the only culturally specific program in the state and region. We run our own African American leadership institute, of which I am proud. I know what we've built will carry on beyond my tenure.

I approach every experience purposefully, contemplating my role and how to contribute value. What is the return on the investment made in me? Reflecting on my leadership journey while writing this book, I observe legacy programs thriving in organizations where I have worked or consulted. Partnerships persist even after a change in leadership, indicating the sustainability of what we created together. These enduring outcomes attest to successfully navigating the change management and vitality challenges I discussed earlier.

Regardless of your field, it is crucial to consider your impact. What tangible results do you have from your positions? What is the return on investment you leave behind? These *receipts* are etched in ink, visible evidence of your contributions. People should be able to discern these marks in you and your work, just as they do in mine. As a self-aware leader, you understand that you align with your purpose, skillfully navigating your narrative.

Finally, the essence of our work always revolves around interactions with people. Our communication leaves a lasting impact, whether physically leading them or communicating through various channels such as phone, text, email, or social media. Leadership, fundamentally, is about people and how we treat one another.

Leadership with Impact

My most remarkable experiences have unfolded while serving on boards and commissions, occupying leadership roles that involve navigating diverse skill sets, backgrounds, personalities, motivations, and understandings. I've encountered mentors and role models in these roles, forged business connections, and made lasting friendships. The way we treat others is what they remember; it's not about what we can gain from them but about establishing a meaningful connection.

In these experiences, I have expanded my expertise from being the arts education lady to being a manager and then a Board Member, nonprofit founder, and consultant. When you ask to work with me, it's important for me to understand you, your experiences and goals, and how we can work together.

Questions for Reflection

- What have you accomplished in your journey?
- What do you aspire to achieve in the future?
- What impact do you intend to make?
- What qualifications do you need to turn your future aspirations into reality?
- What existing resources can you engage with today?

CHAPTER 3

DEFINING YOUR APPROACH WITH PRECISION

"Determination and hard work are as important as talent. Don't let anyone discourage you! Yes, rejection and criticism hurt. Get used to it."

– Judy Blume

It is vital to be self-aware when defining your approach to leadership. If you don't understand who you are as a leader, you can't be effective in your positions, whether in your job, as a Board member, or as a volunteer leader. I learned this from reading John C. Maxwell's book *The Self-Aware Leader*. To that end, I had to figure out my philosophy, approach, and how I led myself before I could effectively lead others.

Along the journey, we forget that leading people starts with ourselves. You can't walk into a room to manage a meeting, be disorganized, and not have at least an idea of how you want to approach the agenda. Or worse, walk into a meeting and have no idea what the agenda is! Long before entering the room, define your approach to leadership. In Maxwell's book, he gives examples of his mistakes leading because he wasn't aware of himself, and I think we can all learn from those lessons.

Maxwell shares from *The Contrarian's Guide to Leadership* by Steven B. Sample, that "The average person suffers from three delusions," to paraphrase: they are a good driver, have a good sense of humor, and are a good listener. Maxwell admits that he's guilty of all three, and it was a coworker that called it to his attention at least on one account. He shared that she confronted him about not listening to others by stating, "John, when people talk to you, often you seem distracted and look around the room. We're not sure you're listening to us."

As hard as it was for him to hear, he immediately apologized, and set out to right the wrong by trying to change.

We can't lead if we aren't abiding by the standards we've set for ourselves and our employees or volunteers. For example, if there is a standard for office attire, we can't show up looking like we just rolled out of bed. We can't tell the accounting department to follow accounting standards if we run two sets of books. It just isn't good leadership if we aren't even leading ourselves.

Much like in their career development, leaders don't all adhere to the same approach, and the same applies to facilitators. Given my experience facilitating workshops, I'm frequently asked how I define my approach.

Three Dimensions of My Approach

Particularly in the equity space, where content delivery can be interpreted in various ways, it is imperative for those hiring me to comprehend who I am, my perspective, and how I convey messages. My approach can be defined in three dimensions.

1. Self-Reflection: As I review the successes and failures of the last ten years, I understand that I need to understand what needs to be changed to progress. Without evaluating myself, I could be delivering old information in an old style that doesn't reflect my current work.
2. Self-Awareness: Knowing my skills and experiences is critical. This allows me to discern whether I am the right person to deliver a specific message.
3. Self-Evaluation: When I think about how I facilitate, I know it doesn't resonate with everyone. I had a client return and ask me to facilitate a workshop because they liked how I captured people's attention via video platform over the course of six hours. That's not easy to do, and I was selected over another presenter because the client appreciated how I facilitate. When I look at other opportunities, I evaluate my skills and experiences versus what they need to see if we're a good fit.

Self-Reflection

When reflecting on your career, consider both your successes and failures. These experiences are crucial in shaping who we become as leaders and facilitators. It's essential to recognize that our achievements and setbacks influence how we interact and navigate with people. While missteps are inevitable, the key is to learn from them and avoid repeating the same errors in the future.

As a facilitator, working with diverse groups—ranging from teams and organizations to large and small gatherings—I contemplate the array of experiences accumulated over time. I then tailor my approach by incorporating the knowledge gained from each interaction. This personalized strategy enables me to design program experiences that effectively resonate with the individuals in the room.

Self-Awareness

Recognizing the value of my skills and experience is the foundation of effective communication when accepting invitations to present to groups. Before committing to any opportunity, I proactively inquire about the topics or learning objectives the hosting party desires. This selectivity stems from my self-awareness, as I don't readily accept every invitation.

While some may choose engagements based on the prestige of a particular company, I prioritize alignment. Before accepting any contract, I assess whether I am the right fit for the opportunity. Knowing where your expertise fits and if it fits the speaking engagement, then recognizing where another speaker may be better suited for the group will best serve the client and those participating. It's not merely about having the right skill set on paper; it's about ensuring my work aligns seamlessly with the client's identity. Otherwise, regardless of my expertise, effective communication becomes challenging.

I believe in understanding my role as either the messenger or not. Even if I possess the appropriate skills on paper, if the audience isn't receptive, it hinders effective communication. I evaluate the client's expectations when considering collaborations, especially in equity work. If their vision conflicts with my approach, leading to potential challenges in facilitating workshops, I will decline the offer.

Self-Evaluation

When I need clarification on partnering with a client, I refer to my checklist or philosophy. The key lies in finding common ground and identifying disparities. Successful facilitation requires alignment in both message and delivery. For example, suppose a client wishes to delve into the discussion of systemic racism, a topic I facilitate. In that case, the focus must extend beyond systems to encompass the people involved.

My Self Evaluation Checklist

1. Why do you think diversity and inclusion matters at the organization?

2. In what ways do you think the organization does a great job at supporting diversity and inclusion?

3. What have you seen work at other companies addressing diversity and inclusion that you'll like to see at the organization?

4. What are the top 3 critical factors for success of equity and inclusion at the organization?

5. How do we ensure there is accountability for improving diversity and inclusion at the organization?

It's a fruitful partnership when the individuals impacted by these systems are emphasized, as understanding and addressing their perspectives are integral to fostering change. To be an effective facilitator, I must explore biases and meet the audience where they currently stand. Starting from their reality, rather than an idealized perception, ensures more impactful and relevant facilitation.

Reflecting on my leadership journey, I realize that the principles of self-awareness and adherence to my philosophy are indispensable for successful partnerships and the facilitation of workshops. This mutual clarity is crucial for clients to identify the facilitator who aligns with their objectives and values.

Questions for Reflection

- How does my self-awareness influence how I approach and evaluate opportunities to present or collaborate, and how does this selectivity contribute to effective communication?
- How do I assess alignment beyond having the proper skill set when considering contracts or collaborations,

and how does this contribute to the success of the communication process?

☞ Reflecting on instances where I have referred to my checklist or philosophy when uncertain about partnering with a client, how has this practice helped me find common ground and ensure alignment in both message and delivery during facilitation?

☞ Think about a time when you were facilitating on a subject that is challenging, how did you handle it? What would you change or what did you change in your approach? What were the results?

CHAPTER 4

IDENTIFYING AND LEVERAGING YOUR ZONE OF GENIUS

> "I found that every time I asked for permission the answer tended to be no, so I had to make my own yeses."
>
> – Issa Rae

What do you think of when you hear the phrase Zone of Genius? To leverage our knowledge and opportunities, we must delve into our competencies. What makes you uniquely YOU? What sparks your interest? What are your passions, skills, and values? Combined, these are your zones of genius, where you shine, and where you can capitalize in your career. As you think about your career and identify your zones, you begin to paint a clearer picture of your leadership identity, guiding the rooms you can confidently enter, lead, and facilitate.

Traditionally, we were ingrained with the notion of addressing weaknesses and striving for improvement. The people at the top of the organization were assumed, perhaps incorrectly, to know everything and be their best selves. The reality, the contemporary thinking, is that we get the most from ourselves and others when we focus on sharpening skills we already have. We can then figure out how to balance a skillset to foster growth. This approach emphasizes identifying your zones of genius and those within your team, recognizing gaps, and strategically filling those spaces with individuals who complement those strengths. Instead of focusing on weakness, we focus on our inherent gifts and talents, leveraging the collective strength of the team to fortify the entire organization.

Discovering Your Zone of Genius

It's all great that we focus on zones of genius, but how do we know where our strengths are? Do we wait until an annual evaluation? Do we have the power to change? What if we are the leaders? Discovering your zone of genius requires introspection.

The person you are today may differ significantly from who you were a year or five years ago. Success demands a pause from relentless pushing and a deliberate reflection on oneself. Your zone of genius materializes where your interests, passions, values, and skills intersect. This convergence empowers you to concentrate on your innate abilities and propel yourself toward success.

YOUR ZONE OF GENIUS

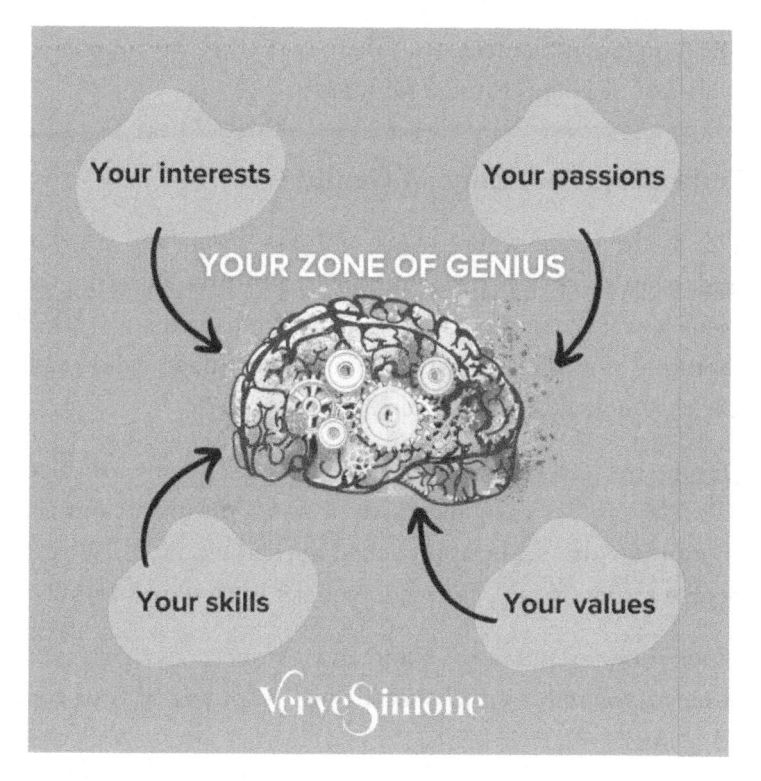

- Your interests
- Your passions
- Your skills
- Your values

VerveSimone

Think of the zone of genius as a Venn diagram. You want to focus on the intersection of passion, interest, skills, and values.

Then, ask your team about themselves. You will begin to gain insight into the unique skills, interests, and talents of others. Where you are weaker, hire someone to support you. Where you are strong, offer that to the team. Be smart about delegating tasks.

As a small business owner, I know I can do my bookkeeping, but it takes me hours and my accountant minutes. An hour of my time is worth more than figuring out expenses and income in accounting software; that's where I hire people. By discovering where we excel and are passionate, we can create a team that complements us. When we do this, we nourish our souls and discover genuine fulfillment.

Embracing Your Zone of Genius

This is the realm where magic unfolds, propelling you into leadership roles and onto speaking platforms. Directing my focus toward my superpowers had a transformative effect, capturing the attention of influential individuals who might not have noticed me otherwise.

During my tenure as the executive at the State of Black Arizona, another executive director noted positive comments about me. Curious, he approached me and inquired, "Why do people respect you?", "How do you get invited in a room?"

When your reputation commands respect even in your absence, you're effectively harnessing the power of your zone of genius.

Four Strategies to Secure Your Spot in the Room

Embracing your zone of genius means you can leverage your experience to discover unexpected opportunities. Opportunities will arise, allowing you to connect with individuals and explore places you might not have anticipated. This stems from your authenticity in acknowledging your strengths and contributions and your commitment to act with integrity in your endeavors.

1. Read the Room: The key to entering any room is authenticity. Understand how to read the room and gauge the appropriate intensity of your true self.

Authenticity is a skill that allows you to be honest, forthright, silly, or quirky, resonating with those who value your genuine nature.

2. Say What You Mean: Integrity is paramount. Following through on commitments, whether accepting or declining opportunities, builds a reputation for reliability. People remember actions and inactions, making it crucial to uphold promises.

3. Follow Through: Commitment without action is hollow. Effective leaders commit to tasks and deliver on promises. A consistent record of follow-through builds trust and establishes you as a reliable individual worth following.

4. Show Up: Timing matters. Being a leader involves discerning when your presence is essential and when delegation is appropriate. Effectiveness lies in understanding the right moments to be actively engaged.

Questions for Reflection

- What are your interests, passions, skills, and values?
- How can you leverage what you've learned and what you're passionate about into your leadership role?
- What adjustments can you make to align with your future goals?
- How can you help your team find their zone of genius?
- How can roles change to facilitate the best in people?

CHAPTER 5

LEVERAGING YOUR CONNECTIONS

"Be Strong, be fearless, be beautiful. And believe that anything is possible when you have the right people there to support you."

– Misty Copeland

Did you know your network of connections has value? Every relationship has a currency associated with it. You've built professional relationships through attending online meetings, in-person events, positions, volunteering, mentoring, and social media sites like LinkedIn. They are like-minded people who serve similar communities to where you serve.

They are your marketing team for your business or nonprofit, your mentors and mentees, your support when needed, and the people with whom you have professional relationships. You may have friends from years ago when you worked with them, people you met last week at a conference, and everything in between. They are your network.

How can you leverage your network? Begin by taking inventory of your network. Just because you go to many networking meetings and have a stack of business cards and LinkedIn contacts does not mean you can leverage those relationships, if you can call them relationships at all. In fact, it's likely many are just contacts and not people you can call or email to ask questions or favors.

Over the years, I have learned that the pickier I am about selecting my network, the better I can build relationships and thus leverage my network. The more I can engage with people, the more likely they are to take my call. For example, I can call a C-suite leader that I have worked with as an employee, board member, volunteer, or consultant and they will answer the phone. It's not all of them, but the ones with whom I have curated a relationship will answer.

I am careful about who I call to ask for favors or to connect to someone else in my network. I've spent time and effort to build authentic relationships and don't want to ruin it with a bad referral. What many people don't realize is that relationships hold value and help us complete tasks and projects, and build other experiences.

And it's not just about what they can offer you. You need to hold value for them as well.

To go where you want to go, you need people. What's your currency to the people that you want to engage in, the work that you need to do? Focus on building those relationships. Just as I ask my network, I am asked by them as well, so I am willing to build relationships outside work to truly get to know them.

The Relationship Couch

My professional network has a seat on my relationship couch, and I hope I have a seat on theirs. We each may interact differently, but we're all together. We may call someone a friend, but they may be acquaintances who support us at work or on a board. My friends may not understand what I do professionally, and that's okay too. Each person with whom we are connected may or may not be on our relationship couch.

- Who is in your network?
- How do you support each other?
- How do you define different people in your network?
- How can you utilize people you know to grow or change your network?
- Who can you leave where they are?

As you review your contacts, think about how you define them. Place them in categories - champion, partner, ally, associate, or a friend, etc. There's likely some overlap. For example, I have friends from work who are also volunteering with me. There are friends I know from high school or college, friends with whom I travel, and others who support my professional career. It is essential to understand who they are and how they contribute to your personal and professional journeys.

You may decide that some folks must be left off your relationship couch. That's okay, too. We need everyone in our lives, but maybe not in our leadership path. Get to know your people, what they bring to your life, and what you can bring to theirs. That's where the magic of networking happens.

You can't do it all. Believe me. I've tried.

I can't run a nonprofit and a consulting business without the support of my relationship couch and experts in the community. This includes hiring professionals for administrative tasks, social media, writing, and editing. I couldn't serve where I serve without my network, and neither can you.

How does your network work for you?

The pandemic put the brakes on in-person networking, but I love that we have found new ways to connect. There are weeks when I feel like I live on web conferences and other weeks when I am driving miles to meet people. I follow up with a few new people I meet to get to know them. I follow up to connect them with people I know, and they connect me to people they know. That's how networking works.

Often in business we are compelled to network, thankfully, after the past few years, people are starting to network in-person again. Many flit aimlessly from meeting to meeting without real thought or plan for action when at the meeting or afterward. If attending meetings is required to run your business, do you really know why or what you should be accomplishing when there?

Stop making promises at any meetings and not following up. I will make it happen when I promise to introduce you to someone. Relationships that I have can change your network just the same as yours can change mine. Without a strategy or intent, networking meetings are a colossal waste of time. It's true that along the way, we find people we like, and they become friends, but it doesn't have to be everyone, nor do I think it should be everyone. And not every meeting or opportunity you hear about is for you.

Take a step back from meetings. Connect with people that you've met recently. Whether it's a note on a LinkedIn request, an email, or setting up a one-to-one meeting, make it happen because pouring time into those relationships is essential.

1. Define relationships. What does each person mean to you?
2. Grow new relationships. Who have you met recently that you'd like to get to know more deeply? Make it happen.
3. Networking is about give-and-take. They may need something today, and you may need something tomorrow. That's how it works. The quality of people in your network will legitimize you as a professional

and your body of work. A good referral can go a long way toward creating a valuable professional relationship.

Are you willing to do that the next time you are asked to volunteer? Small moments like these allow you to activate your network through relationships you've already built. Remember, it's not always about literally giving and taking, whether of your time or experience, but about how you interact with people that makes it meaningful for both of you.

Don't be the kind of person who hands out their business cards and runs away. That will never work to build a meaningful relationship. I will tell you now that I will not partner with you unless we've had time to get to know each other and/or the organization you represent. If you're simply handing out cards, you're building transactional relationships alongside a pile of business cards. That's not how leaders are made.

Leaders build relationships with other leaders, with their teams, and within the community they serve. These are long-lasting relationships that have been developed over time and experience. It can't all be transactional if you want your network to work with you and be strong.

People only hear from you when you want something, and they only interact with you when it makes sense for their gain. Also, your return on investment (ROI) should be on both sides. I like to look at this as a teeter-totter.

When I am in a professional relationship with a person, I think about how the scale is balanced. If one is not balanced with the other, your relationship may have some challenges. It's like a group project where a couple of people are doing all the work, and the others are sitting around not adding value but expecting the same grade. It just doesn't work well in the long term.

The relationship should instead be evolving. The number of teeters and totters should be equal over time. In this way, each person sees their value and recognizes the value of their partner.

Your network works when you can pick up the phone and ask for a favor. If you have a problem, you know who to call to either listen, or to solve it; that's an effective network. If you can't do that, you need to review your network and decide who you need to fill the gaps.

As you sort through your relationship couch, remember that relationships change. While some can weather growing pains, others may not. By being self-aware, you can make changes and adjust your network. You will also have long-term relationships that change over time but stay connected.

Questions for Reflection

1. Who is part of your network?
2. Who do you need or want in your network?
3. How can your current network connect you to the people you want to meet?

CHAPTER 6

GUIDING PEOPLE AND TEAMS

> "When you're in your lane there's no traffic."
>
> – Ava Duvernay

Leading teams has been an integral part of my career development. This is where we, as leaders, can make the most impact. Start from where you are today—set goals. Find people and resources. And keep leading. For me, leading is about listening to the team, finding out their needs, and connecting with the community we serve.

In this chapter, I share different ways I have led teams so you can get to know me and begin to see your own path.

One-to-One or None

I am a leader who likes to have one-to-one meetings so I can get to know my staff. I ask what they expect in a leader and their needs, and I may also share my needs. I want to understand where people are coming from (their positionality) so that we can begin to develop working relationships. This way, I understand who is on my team, where we begin, and where we can go together.

After I do that, I think about how I take the people on the journey, whether they're in the right seat on the bus, or not. A person in development may be better suited to marketing, or the opposite could be true. Sometimes, I may have to let someone go because they aren't the right fit for the need. That's not an easy decision, but as a leader, it is one of many that must be addressed.

My goal is to see how the team can best operate because the team is only as good as the members on the team. One of my first leadership opportunities with a large team came at a local nonprofit in the Metropolitan Phoenix area. I was in my twenties, leading about ten people in programs. It was challenging and necessary for me to listen, learn, and reflect as I walked through the experience. To get to know them better, I chose a book to set the tone *Who Moved My Cheese* by Dr. Spencer Johnson, which became our theme. We read and studied the book together for a year.

On the first anniversary, my team made me a clay model cheese with a little person in it. I realized they could communicate with me about their leadership journeys. They were also open to innovative ideas because we had framed the story around the book and communicated in those terms. For me, it was an effective way to meet the team where they were and bring them forward in a way that made us all comfortable and open to change.

Next is Coaching

Now that we understand who is on the bus, we need to decide how the bus will move. How do I coach people to do their part to get things moving? That comes in different forms. For me, I utilize my StrengthsFinder® characteristics of individuality. That means giving each person on the bus what they need and recognizing they don't all need the same coaching.

This type of coaching might seem like I favor one person over another, but I have to give the people what they need in the organization's context and expectations to bring out their best self. I must meet people where they are as individuals, and some people need more of something. Some people need the opportunity to be motivated.

At the beginning of my career, what I found challenging was when the team changed from experienced career employees to more emerging career employees in the field. It was then that I adjusted how I was leading the team. We selected to use a different book as our guide, *The Five Dysfunctions of a Team* by Patrick Lencioni.

You may have cringed at the word dysfunction, and that's okay. What I like about this book and the leadership style is that the author focuses on understanding a pyramid. The organization must be focused on trust, conflict resolution, commitment, accountability, and tangible results.

If we don't have trust, then we have conflict. If we have poor performance, we have high team member turnover. If there is a lack of commitment, we have absenteeism and revisit topics repeatedly.

With a few pieces working, some good can happen. When we focus on all aspects, we get greater results, and people want to stay on the team. That takes a commitment to the organization's mission, but a lack of trust between members can hinder the process.

I focused the team on building trust, and we began to work better together. That's where I saw the team was lacking, so that's where we focused. Your team might be different, so you should focus on where they need leadership. You may choose a different model to follow, and that's entirely up to you. I wanted to give you examples as a place to start, so you can find your footing and your voice as a leader.

Leading Volunteers

As a Trustee of the Desert Botanical Garden, I undertook a specific project focused on one of my passions, age diversification. The strategy was to increase the number of 25- to 40-year-olds who came to the gardens. At the time, that was an audience of interest but not intentionally executed, nor was it a place who individuals of this age group thought to go.

We found that you might take your grandmother to the garden, but it was not where you saw yourself. In that leadership role, I was not leading employees, they were volunteers. I was leading professionals like myself at the management, C-suite, or executive levels. Together, we were working to accomplish something for the organization. In doing so, while I didn't lead this group with a book, it was still a framework where I utilized their time, talents, and treasures.

While leading this team was different, I was able to parlay my skills and experience to drive us to our goal. I asked for their talents and treasures for a certain amount of time. The ten members of this board committee and I solved the issue and got more visitors in the newly targeted age group.

We went through surveys, focus groups, hosted events, and more to accomplish our goal. Ultimately, the effort became a board-appointed committee, which could serve as a succession plan for the board. The Monarch Council is still in existence.

While I still serve as a Trustee but for the foundation, I look from afar at the legacy continuing to move forward. Ultimately, that board-appointed committee became leaders who interacted with other board members regarding their talents. They could sit on committees where they were a voice, a fresh perspective, and a different generation with a seat at the table planning for the future of the garden with the current board members.

Each leadership experience as a volunteer has helped me grow as a leader. Through self-reflection, I have learned how to work with people of different backgrounds in varied stages of their leadership and volunteer journeys.

Leading a National Team

My approach to leading teams revolves around attentive listening at the outset—understanding the individual needs of team members and the organizational requirements. I believe in fostering learning by establishing a framework or theme that propels us forward. Additionally, I emphasize reflective support throughout the process, ensuring effective leadership as we navigate the path ahead.

As the board chair of a regional arts organization, currently called Western States Arts Federation (WESTAF), I am responsible for leading, with 25 other professionals, the Board of Trustees, a $12 million organization representing 13 states and 3 pacific territories. Each year, we meet three times in various places such as Alaska, Denver, and identified rural communities. My leadership approach is facilitated by a tool I call The Three-Legged Stool: governance, visioning, and community.

1. Governance is frequent and transparent communication that provides comprehension insight into all aspects of the organization to further the progress of and ensures accountability, performance, and fiduciary oversight.
2. Visioning is focused around select, key strategic planning, projects, and initiatives that utilize the breadth and depth of expertise represented within the board for organization.
3. Community means we make space for learning and reflection while spending time with each other to deepen working relationships and networks. This builds knowledge and understanding for better decision making to the organization at all levels.

The Three-Legged Stool

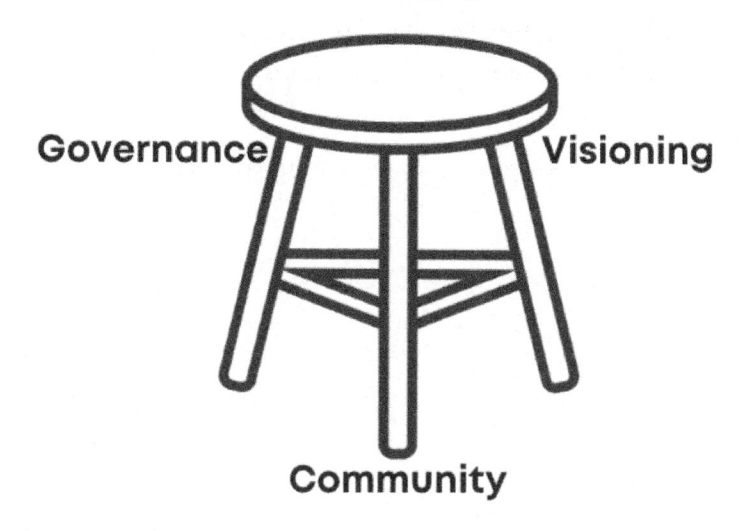

Governance   **Visioning**

Community

With 25 board members spanning different states, we transitioned from local arts administrators, consultants and business professionals in various regions. I introduced this tool to guide this diverse group. The visual representation was prominently displayed in our board book.. This facilitates our collective understanding of governance, visioning, and community.

Leading volunteers may be different from leading others so you may need, or want, to take a step back to evaluate yourself and others. Then you can begin to lead people in the direction of the organization.

Questions for Reflection

- What's your leadership style?
- How do you lead different teams?
- Where is your team struggling?
- What does your team need from you to be successful?

CHAPTER 7

HANDLING CHALLENGES WITH GRACE

> "Fear is boring."
>
> — **Elizabeth Gilbert**

When leaders discuss challenging situations, it's common for many of us to react with negativity or anxiety. Frequently, I'm asked how I approach conflict with composure. My essential advice to you is to shift your mindset. Instead of dwelling on the negative emotions, pinpoint the issue's core. Whether it stems from a lingering problem with a past manager, a misalignment of your implemented style with team dynamics, or another source, it's crucial to identify the root cause of the conflict. Only then can you initiate the process of resolution and move forward.

The problem won't resolve itself.

When I was early into a leadership role at a local nonprofit, I had my first significant number of staff members. One had lost a family member and was completely checked out at work;

they weren't talking to anyone. At that point in my career, I wasn't equipped to do anything except give them space.

I entered their office and started a dialogue that ended with them being hostile toward me. What I didn't realize at the time was that when a person is grieving, they have a range of emotions that may or may not have anything to do with me or anyone else at work.

Today, I would approach the situation with more empathy and understanding of their emotional state. Instead of trying to initiate a conversation that might lead to further stress, I'd let them know I'm available to listen whenever they're ready to talk. I would also offer professional resources, such as counseling services, and assure them that their feelings are valid and make sure they knew they were supported. This approach not only respects their space but also provides them with options to seek help if they choose.

What I didn't realize for the first six months in that leadership role was that there was another staff person who was supposed to be my second in command. One evening she entered my office and told me I wasn't utilizing her in her role. Turns out, she was told she had the role but I hadn't been told by my predecessor. It was a lightbulb moment for me! People want to be involved and as a leader, I need to talk to them to understand staff and for them to also understand my approach. Sometimes we each need to adjust so we can all work together.

There also will be times when the best solution is to walk away. Sometimes a job isn't a good fit for you or you aren't a good fit for the organization. If you come into an organization seeking to make changes and there are individuals resistant to change, it may not be the right place for you.

One organization might want only to see situations through their lens of control. In some situations they may want that because there could be things happening they don't want anyone to know. That's not a place I want to be and not an organization that is open to change. Always consider a place you can be seen, heard and valued otherwise you will spend your wheels questioning your worth and that is a hindrance to your professional growth.

I chalk all of these up to experiences, but being aware can help you to faster recognize when situations demand a change in practice, approach, or another solution. There are people who don't want to be led and leaders who don't want change. It's just the way it is, and if conversations can't get you to see eye-to-eye, then it isn't a good fit; it's time to find a new place to showcase your skills and experience. When I look back, I see how these experiences have shaped me as a leader.

From a relational perspective, navigating conflict is akin to being in a troubled relationship where you know issues need addressing. Avoiding the conversation only allows the problem to fester, eventually becoming a more significant threat to the relationship. Eventually, you recognize the need to confront the issues, even if it leads to a breakup.

The same principle applies to conflicts faced by leaders. Ignoring the problem won't make it disappear, no matter how long it's avoided. As leaders, acknowledging this reality empowers us to address the issue and its underlying causes. Leaders cannot afford to be conflict-averse; instead, they must proactively gather individuals involved, then tackle and resolve the issue.

The 24-Hour Rule

Not every conflict requires an instant response; many times, the wisest course of action is to "sleep on it." Let it sit for a bit of time, then come back to it with a fresh perspective to confront the problem. This is what I refer to as the 24-Hour Rule. Create the expectation that not every question in every meeting needs an immediate response. Give space, and grace, for people to think about their decisions. My approach looks like this:

1. Allow time for dialogue.
2. Ensure all levels or positions are open and heard.
3. Provide an opportunity to raise concerns.
4. Permit silent moments in difficult conversations before someone responds.
5. Manage the desire for shutdowns or walking out.
6. Allow for breathing and thinking.
7. Establish psychological safety.
8. Give the grace to revisit and address things that have been said after reactions have occurred.

This allows everyone to be heard and respected. Some people are quiet thinkers while others want to talk it out; both are okay. When I have taken time to develop an answer or solution, the result is more impactful. I am more confident in the decision. Over time, I've learned this can be the best approach.

At my workshops, I tell attendees it is okay to be silent and have silence in session for a while. It sometimes makes people uncomfortable but it also gives everyone time to think and formulate a response which is important for everyone to have the opportunity to voice their opinion and be heard.

For those who process information faster, this approach can be frustrating, so this approach can offer the opportunity to practice patience. Immediate action can be more reactive than solution-oriented, and create unwanted drama. By waiting, I grant myself and my team the opportunity to assess the situation, contemplate the root of the problem, and devise constructive, actionable solutions.

I often apply this approach to emails I receive that strike me as peculiar. As a leader within the organization, the temptation to be a keyboard warrior and hastily respond may be strong, but I recognize that it isn't effective. Instead, I revisit the email the following day, posing questions to myself such as:

- What is the sender communicating?
- How can I respond in a way that creates a dialogue?
- How can we navigate as a team?

Navigating difficult situations is truly about tone. Sometimes, it's not what you say; it's how you're saying it that is effective. If I am open to conversation, we can get farther than if I am not. Even when it is challenging, I want to understand the root of the issue and begin to address it promptly.

As leaders, we muster the confidence to listen and then respond.

- ☞ How am I reading the room?
- ☞ Can this be resolved by phone call, video conference, or does it require an in-person meeting?
- ☞ Does the response need to be in writing?

Navigating conflict with poise is about communication: sometimes it will take a series of conversations and a workshop; other times, an email response will do; still others might require a phone call or meeting. Depending on the situation, it may be an apology or accepting responsibility that will satisfy people. While you may continue to disagree with the person, it's important to make apologies genuine without reigniting an argument.

That being said, conflict isn't always negative. Initially, it may seem like a negative situation, but again, it may not. It may not be nebulous ambiguity, either. Sometimes, it is what I like to call "good ambiguity" from which we can learn and grow. I think of this like a diamond needing pressure to form.

The Diamond Leader

If you're going to be a diamond leader, you've got to be ready to manage the pressure of conflict. My experience has been that the best relationships have come out of the times when we were at odds or walking through a challenging situation.

- ☞ Are we willing to work together for the greater good?
- ☞ Are you staying mad at each other?
- ☞ Do we need to break up?

How you react under pressure says a lot about you as a leader. I still respect the other person when discussing times when we've agreed or disagreed. I am more comfortable being honest and transparent because of the trust we've developed over time.

Questions for Reflection

- What is the root of the issue?
- What is the best way to resolve the issue?
- Are you willing to communicate about ways to resolve the issue?

CONCLUSION

MY LEADER, MY SELF

> "The only courage you ever need is the courage to fulfill the dreams of your own life. But if you don't have a dream today, start dreaming."
>
> – **Oprah Winfrey**

It is my sincere hope that you have found this book helpful as you continue your leadership journey. Finding your superpower takes time, self-reflection, a few trials and errors, and a bit of awkward silence at a meeting. That's all part of the journey.

While we can look forward and think about where we'd like to be in a month, quarter, year, or five years, it is essential to reflect often about past experiences. The leader you are today is different from the leader you were last year or last decade, or maybe even last quarter. Keep testing methods of defining and acting on leadership models until you find what works for you and how you need to adjust for different surroundings or people with which you engage. Take what you learn as you develop your voice and style.

CONCLUSION

Identify your strengths and weaknesses, and build a team that compliments you, your background, skills, and experiences. Perhaps you need to speak up. Or perhaps you need to stay silent until the right people are in the room.

What are you doing that makes a positive impact? Will that way work in a different position or volunteer opportunity? Do you lead the same in business as you do when you're leading volunteers or on a board? Even if it's different, are you being true to who you are and who you want to be as a leader? If you're not sure, take time to identify a person or people in your network who can listen and mentor you.

It is in the moments of self-reflection that we can harness our superpowers, understand how to develop others, and to impact those we serve.

ABOUT THE AUTHOR

Teniqua Broughton has more than 20 years of experience in the nonprofit sector, igniting creativity and challenging mediocrity to drive desired outcomes through public speaking and facilitating workshops focused on nonprofit governance, leadership empowerment, and equity readiness.

In 2014, she established VerveSimone Consulting to build an organization that would allow her to control the results of her work. Broughton aimed to expand her capacity and use her influence as a community leader to address issues and topics close to her heart: arts and culture, women and girls, and underrepresented communities. Today, VerveSimone continues to lead change by positively affecting partnerships within the community, as evidenced by her leadership in nonprofit formation and capacity building from inception to scale. Her partnerships include the State of Black Arizona (SBAZ), Arizona Impact for Good, and the Arizona Opera: LOUD! (Living Opera Understanding Diversity). She also organizes and facilitates a variety of leadership workshops focused on equity readiness coaching and assessments that result in organizational strategy recommendations.

Broughton curated a space for seven statewide leadership development groups, from Valley Leadership to Greater Tucson Leadership, committing to developing a shared curriculum on racial justice. Her vision empowers leaders to have honest conversations about the communities in which they live, work, play, and how they, as Arizonans, can engage to make them stronger. She has led the change in equitable grant-making practices as the commissioner chair of the City of Phoenix Arts and Culture Commission. Additionally, she executed the transition of leading a new curriculum for the SBAZ's African American Leadership Institute from Valle de Sol and launched the inaugural institute in Southern Arizona. She currently serves as the chair of the Western States Arts Federation's (WESTAF) Board of Trustees, a board member of the Desert Botanical Garden Foundation, ASU Knowledge Exchange for Resilience (KER) Council, and she is a member of the LISC Phoenix's Local Advisory Committee, Intuit's Small Business Council and the National Small Business Association Leadership Council.

Broughton has been awarded the Phoenix Titan 100 of Industry in 2022 and 2023, recognized as a titan, a person of exceptional importance and reputation in their industry. Most recently, she was named in AZ Big Media's 50 Business Leaders to Watch in 2024, received the 2023 NCBW's Economic Empowerment Legend Award, and was honored by the Arizona Capitol Times as one of the Women Achievers of Arizona. In 2021, she received the Arizona State University MLK Servant Leader- Leadership Award and was a Phoenix Business Journal's 2021 Most Admired Leader recipient. In 2017, her peers selected her as the recipient of the Arizona Champion Award for the Central Arizona region from the Flinn Foundation's Arizona Center for Civic Leadership for her significant contributions to civic leadership.

She holds a master's degree in education with a focus on Educational Administration and Supervision from Arizona State University and a bachelor's degree in educational psychology with an emphasis on theater for youth from the same institution. Broughton is a certified Nonprofit Accounting Professional (CNAP) and holds certificates in Nonprofit Leadership and Management from the University of Arizona and Boston College, as well as in Equity and Inclusion from the Nonprofit Leadership Alliance.

Made in the USA
Las Vegas, NV
04 March 2025